CW00435309

# Golden Nuggets

## Donnie Black

*Donnie Black*

# Contents

# Autumn

I f you haven`t already noticed the lovely colours of the trees and bushes in season, take a moment to observe the beauty of the variety of colours which are displayed, all around us on our doorstep, during the autumn season.

The leaves turn into various colours in the autumn which shows us a glory at the end of their lives. Shortly after this beautiful display the leaves fall one by one, to the ground. Their short life has come to an end.

There is a verse in the bible. It`s in the Old Testament with a big, strange name called Ecclesiastes. In chapter 3v1-2 it says: There is a time for everything. A time to be born and a time to die.

In the spring of the year a new leaf emerges from a bud which looked very dead during the winter. It`s great to see new life appearing after the long cold winter season. A time to be born.

A short summer period of life, and autumn arrives as our Bible verse says. A time to die.

Our own lives can be likened to the leaves. A time to be born and a time to die.

Each person who reads this verse knows they were born but uncertain when the time to die will come.

Nevertheless, each one of us, no matter our outward appearance can approach death with a glory and a beauty which has to do with our character, i.e. who we really are.

This lovely poem by Amy Carmichael captures it so beautifully.

> Great Giver of my lovely green in spring,
>
> A dancing singing green upon my tree,
>
> My green has passed; I have no song to sing,
>
> What will my Autumn be?
>
> Must it be, though alive, as all but dead,
>
> A heavy footed and a silent thing?
>
> Effectless, sapless, tedious, limited,
>
> A withered vanishing?
>
> Thus I; but He to me: Have I not shown
>
> In Autumn woodland and on mountain fell,
>
> The splendour of My purpose for Mine own?
>
> Fear not for all is well.
>
> And thou shalt see, My child, what I will do,
>
> For as thy lingering Autumn days unfold,
>
> The lovely, singing green of hitherto
>
> Will come to you in gold.

When we surrender our lives to Jesus and invite Him into our hearts, we receive His eternal life, so that even when our short life here on earth is over, we will go to be with Him forever. We can go out of this life in a blaze of glory even greater than the leaves.

It`s the beautiful life of the Lord Jesus Christ in us which makes all the difference, as to whether we have a sad and sorry ending, or one of glory.

I pray that you will take time, while you have it, to prepare to meet God as Amos 4v12 says.

You might be in the autumn days of your life even although you are still young.

# Ask, Seek, Knock

The young man paid a visit to the doctor. He was a bit nervous and shy. The doctor inquired of him what his problem was. He mentioned a few things which the doctor addressed by prescribing some medication.

When the man got back to the car, he remembered that there was something else which he should have told the doctor. Because he hadn`t asked for help in this area of addiction he didn`t receive help for this problem.

When Jesus said to a blind man, "what do you want me to do for you?" the blind man said, "I want to receive my sight" (Mark 10: 51).

What would you say to Jesus if He asked, "What would you like me to do for you?"

Matthew 7:7 encourages us to Ask, Seek and Knock. We are assured that our Father in heaven will give good things to those who ask Him (v.11).

Thought would need to go into the answer, because the motive for asking is open to challenge. You might not receive because of a wrong motive (James 4:3).

One thing is certain: God gives grace to the humble (James 4:6). Let`s all ask for grace and allow our heavenly Doctor to heal our wounds. Let`s make sure we don`t forget to mention a particular problem. Tell Him everything.

One more thing.

We should rejoice in the Lord always with thanksgiving when we talk to him about our problems, so that we will experience His peace (Philippians 4:4–7)

# *Deceived*

I t was an exciting time for the baby turtles. They had been buried in the sand, on the beach, in the form of an egg for some time. Their development inside of the shell was now complete. It was time for the baby turtles to break out of the shell and dig their way to the surface.

Nature is a wonder to behold. The timing of the turtles hatching coincides with a bright moon which reflects on the sea which gives direction for the newly hatched turtles to find their way into it. The sea is to be their new home where many live to a great old age.

Sadly, because of development in the area near where the turtles hatch, bright lights from the town on the opposite side, away from the sea, cause huge problems for the young turtles.

The confusion begins as soon as the eyes of the turtle see the light.

Which light to follow?

Towards the town or towards the sea?

The turtle so close to the ground has no way of knowing which way to go. It can`t see what's up ahead.

Sadly, many head off in the wrong direction and end up in the town.

They have been deceived by the wrong light.

Many of them die as a result of falling into street drains or being crushed by the wheels of cars and lorries. Some even get trapped in plastic containers and the like left lying around. Once they get in, they are trapped and can`t get out.

Just like nature has provided the light of the moon to shine on the sea at the right time to lead the young turtles in the right direction, so also has God, who is creator of all, provided a light for us to guide us in the right direction.

Psalm 119v105 says, your word is a lamp to my feet and a light to my path.

In John 8v12, when Jesus is speaking, He says, I am the light of the world; he who follows me shall not walk in the darkness but shall have the light of life.

Just as there is a problem for the young turtles deciding which way to go, so also young people and older ones too can be deceived and go in the wrong direction.

Many people get caught up in traps of drugs, alcohol, and pornography. Also anger, resentment, and bitterness are the result of going in the wrong direction.

Proverbs 14 v12: There is a way that seems right to a

man but the end of it are the ways of death.

I would like to point you in the right direction today. Ask Jesus into your heart and let Him be your guide. He said, I am the Way the Truth and the Life, no one comes to the Father but by Me. John 14 v 6. Jesus will lead you, not only to the sea which is meant to be the turtle's home but beyond the sea of this life into your eternal home in Heaven.

I have set before you this day both life and death. Choose life. Deuteronomy 30v19

# A letter to God

Dear God,

I know I am not the perfect person I should be.

I have done wrong and have failed at times to do what I knew to be right.

Thank you for the forgiveness you offer me.

I believe your Son Jesus paid the debt I owe you.

Thank you,

Your child.

# Reunited

T he two lambs got more and more distressed as the day went on.

They had become separated from their mother in the morning. It was now late evening. Somehow, they had got into a field on the other side of a wire fence.

They were getting very hungry, and mother was getting anxious because she had a lot of milk to feed them with and was feeling uncomfortable by this time.

Although the lambs could see their mother and she could see them through the wire fence, there was no way for them to get together. The fence was a barrier between them.

They could see each other all day but not make contact. It was a sad and distressing situation.

Fortunately, the shepherd noticed the problem and set about sorting it.

He went and did something that the sheep and lambs could not do. He opened a gate to let the lambs be reunited with their mother. Oh the joy of seeing the hungry lambs satisfy their thirst and the mother`s relief as she was able to give away her milk.

All we like sheep (lambs) have gone astray, and our sins and iniquities have separated us from God (Isaiah 53:6; 59:2).

Christ died for our sins, to bring us to God, who says, "Return unto me; for I have redeemed you." (1 Peter 3:18; Isaiah 44:22).

Just as we rejoice over the sheep and her lambs, so there is joy in heaven over one sinner who repents (Luke 15:7).

Have you been reunited yet with our Father in heaven?

The gate is open wide. Jesus opened it for us when He died on the cross.

Thank you, Jesus.

# Lessons from a Garden Hose

One day I discovered an old garden hose buried underneath a hedge on the edge of a field.

I thought that if I could rescue it from the ground, it could be useful on the farm where I worked.

I set about pulling it out from the soil and grass which were holding it captive where it had been for a very long time. Hedge roots had also got a grip of it.

Eventually I had salvaged a length of about 50 yards.

After a bit of cleaning up and straightening, I was able to put this garden hose to good use.

During the wintertime when the frost was very severe, the water pipes in some of the byres where the cows were kept, would freeze up and the cows would get thirsty.

To solve the problem quickly, rather than try and thaw out the pipes, I connected the garden hose to the tap in the Farmhouse which still had a water supply. The joy of seeing thirsty cows having their thirst quenched was a real treat indeed.

Like the garden hose, we too can be rescued from entanglement in sinful ways by Jesus who said, "The

Son of Man came to seek and to save that which was lost." Luke 19:10

The hymn writer put it nicely,

*I was sinking deep in sin*

*sinking to rise no more*

*Overwhelmed by guilt within*

*Mercy I did implore*

*Then the master of the sea*

*Heard my despairing cry*

*Christ my Saviour lifted me*

*Now safe am I.*

If you ask Jesus to rescue you from your sins, which are entangling you like the garden hose, He will put your life to more use than a hose. He can bless other people as you allow His love to flow through you. You will be blessed also as Proverbs 11:25 says, "He that waters shall be watered also himself."

# Marriage Bliss

**M**y wife and I had enjoyed over 40 years of marriage when one day she said that she would like to have a few hens in our back garden.

This didn`t seem to be a problem at first sight as we had a lot of space in our garden at the back of the house. We live in a cottage in the country.

There was a problem, and it was with me.

You see, I had seen enough of hens. I was born and brought up on a farm where hens were very much a part of everyday life. They wondered around the farm all over the place. That was OK because we could gather eggs from various places among the farm machinery, and wee spaces between the bales of hay and straw. It was good fun and exciting.

The problem was in the evening when it was time to lock the hens away into the henhouse to protect them from the fox.

Some hens naturally retire to bed when it starts to get dark, but others go and hide in awkward places. The worst place was under the henhouse. A long stick was needed to dislodge sleepy hens from their illegal overnight parking lot.

My brothers and I, with anybody else who was around at the time, were encouraged, with a lot of persuasion, to get out there and round up all the unruly hens. We hated that task.

So, when my wife said she would like to have a few hens in our back garden I didn`t show the enthusiasm right away that she was looking for, but love suffers long and is kind (1Corithians 13:4). I love my wife and like to be kind.

I tucked her desire away in the back of my mind. Right away at the very back, but not totally ignored.

God moves in a mysterious way His wonders to perform. One day we were together in a garden centre. There, in a small area set apart for pets, would you believe it? Hens – yes, a few hens. There were also small henhouses in packs that could fit into the back of the car.

The Lord touched my heart. Vision of hens in our back garden began to unfold. I could see the area in my mind where we could place the henhouse. I would dig a trench around the enclosure and secure wire netting into it to stop the fox digging under and killing the hens. My heart really began to warm to the whole project.

We bought and brought home the wee henhouse. I began to put it together as soon as I could. From on the Internet, I ordered some wire netting. While waiting for it to arrive I started to dig the trench for it.

The joy I began to experience as I was engaged in all this activity was unique. It was a joy from the Lord.

You see I had sacrificed my selfish will to please someone else, my wife.

In due course we bought four hens, which gave us four eggs each day for a long time to come.

The scripture came to me in power. "Husbands, love your wives even as Christ loved the Church and gave himself for it (Ephesians 5:25).

I found that the small sacrifice I made for my wife was an illustration of the tremendous sacrifice Christ made for us when he laid down His life for us on the cross, to give us so much more than a few hens, the wonderful gift of Eternal Life with Him in heaven.

For the joy that was set before Him He endured the cross, despised its shame, and has sat down at the right hand of the throne of God (Hebrews 12:2).

J O Y

Jesus first. Others next. Yourself last.

The key to marriage bliss is LOVE.

Prayer: Lord, help us to love others the way you love us. Help us to look for ways to bless others and look less to our own wants. In Jesus name we ask. Amen

# One Vision Only

After collecting a few items at the garden centre, I made my way to the check-out.

I chose one where a lady was almost finished paying for her items, or so I thought.

Just while I was priding myself for a good choice of till with a small queue, a friend of the lady in front of me joined her with a full basket of stuff.

My first thought was, if I had known this was about to happen, I would have chosen another till. I struggled a bit for a few moments until my blood pressure began to fall and then I remembered that all things work together for good to those who love God, to those who are called according to his purpose (Romans 8:28).

Character is developed when we accept adverse circumstances and let them mould us. Patience is often needed throughout the day and will grow as we exercise it.

As I said earlier, I might have chosen a different till to pay my money at if I had known there was going to be a problem at the one I went to.

John tells us that Jesus, knowing all that was

going to happen to him, went forward to meet his enemies, who would take him to be crucified (18:4).

He had One Vision Only and that was to do His Father's will.

Matthew 26v39 says Jesus prayed in the garden of Gethsemane, knowing he was going to die a horrible death on the cross, for our sins, He prayed to His Father, your will be done, not mine.

Prayer: Father help us to choose your will in all circumstances and not look for the easy way if it's not yours. In Jesus name. Amen

# The Illegal Fish

Sometime ago my wife and I were in Australia visiting our son. One day he suggested that we launch his boat and go out onto the river and do a bit of fishing. My wife, who doesn't like being on boats, stayed back at the house. My son, two grandsons, aged 10 and 6, and I eventually got the boat into the water after a half-hour drive to the river.

Fishing went well. I caught one and was very pleased with myself until my son measured it with a ruler. He said it was too small. Apparently, there is a law regarding what size of fish you are allowed to keep. If you are caught ashore with fish that are too small you will be fined. I didn`t want to break the law and go back home with an illegal fish, so I reluctantly let it go back into the river.

This fishing experience led me to think of times in our lives, while we are going about our daily duties, when thoughts come to us, and we hook them just like we do with a fish.

Good and bad thoughts come into our boat (mind). We need to measure them by God`s standard, the rule of love. God is the law giver and our Judge

(Isaiah 33:22). He measures each thought that we have in our mind as each moment passes.

An example of an illegal thought would be inordinate anger, bitterness or resentment.

If we were to allow anything of that nature to live in our heart, God's law of love would demand that we put it back where it belongs – into the river where it came from.

Matthew 22:37–39 is God`s measure or ruler for our behaviour. We are to love God with all our heart, soul and mind, and our neighbour as ourselves.

It was a bit disappointing for me to let go of the fish I had caught. It can be a whole lot harder to let go of sin, which is a title for a huge net filled with immoral things. Galatians 5:19–21 lists a lot of these things.

Some fish can leap high out of the water as they swim along at a fast speed. I saw a video clip where fish were actually landing in the boat. One slapped a man on the side of his face. This illustrates how random thoughts can enter our minds, and we need to be on our guard to make sure no immoral ones get a chance to stay there.

Galatians 5:22–23 indicates where to go fishing for the legal fish. The big ones. Ones you can keep with no fear of breaking the law when you meet the lawgiver. There is no law to break when you come to shore with your boat full of Love, Joy, Peace, Long-suffering, Gentleness, Goodness, Faithfulness, Meekness and Self-control.

Is that a legal thought you have at this moment? He is watching.

# Sacrifice

The gathering of around thirty people sat down to a delicious Christmas meal.

The turkey was succulent and tender.

I don`t know if anyone gave thought to the fact that the turkey had its life taken away from it, by a power beyond its control, so that people could enjoy a good meal.

Jesus also died, but not by a power beyond His control. He willingly gave up his life for our salvation: "I lay down my life for the sheep" (John 10:15).

And a few verses later: "I have power to lay down my life and power to take it again" (v.18).

Have you said, "Thank you, Jesus," for dying for me?

# The Broken Storage Box

**F**our days after Christmas it was time to tidy up around the house.

Large plastic boxes seemed to be the answer to store some of the items that had found their way into the house over the Christmas period. Lots of presents, but also some items that we have been storing for friends, had taken up space in the house but could be safely stored in the garage now.

The shops were very busy as my wife, and I checked out a few different stores looking for the best deal.

We found what we wanted at a good price, lifted three large plastic boxes; made sure we had lids to fit, then made our way to the checkout and paid for the items.

It was a good distance to carry those boxes back to the car, so my arms were quite tired by the time we reached it and it was a great relief when we finally drove home to relax.

Next morning, I was very enthusiastic about helping to get the house in order.

I gathered together some of the items that were to be stored in the garage, and took them there, where the boxes were waiting to get filled.

Sadly, as I separated the boxes, one of them was badly broken. We hadn`t noticed it while the three of them were all together.

I decided to take it back to the shop and get another one.

While carrying it back to the shop, the brokenness of the box made me think of the many people who are broken at this very moment. There are many lives broken because of sin.

The most serious aspect of brokenness is our broken relationship with God.

The bible tells us in Romans 5:12 that "as by one man sin entered into the world and death by sin, and so death passed upon all men, for all have sinned."

Sin separates people from one another causing broken relationships.

It separates husbands and wives, partners, fathers and sons, mothers and daughters, brothers and sisters, teachers and pupils, governments and the people, countries with other countries but most of all, sin is against God. We have all broken His laws which have caused our relationship with Him to become broken and needs to be mended.

It was a bit of an inconvenience for me to have to go all the way back to the shop to swap the plastic box for another one. It was about a twelve-mile round trip as I live in the country out of town.

Nevertheless, I got a new one with no problem.

God sees our brokenness and longs to fix it for us, He sent His Son Jesus into the world to die for us. He took all our sins upon Himself, taking the blame for them as if He had committed the sins. (See, 2 Corinthians 5:12.)

Psalm 147:3 and Isaiah 61:1 tell us that Jesus came to bind up the broken hearted

He can fix our brokenness if we let Him come into our lives.

The small inconvenience I had to get a new box was nothing compared to what God had to do for us. He came from Heaven to earth, became a baby, lived a perfect life, suffered and died on the cross, was buried and raised again and went back to Heaven having finished the work He came to do.

Every year we celebrate Christmas, I often wonder how many people join in the celebrations yet only a few days later are still broken hearted?

Although Christmas comes and goes, God's gift of salvation from sin is being offered continually.

Revelation 3:20. Jesus says, I stand at the door and knock, if anyone hears my voice and opens the door I will come in and sup with him and he with me.

He is knocking at your heart's door right now and will come in if you let Him.

He will fix your broken relationship with God and with other people and bring peace into your heart where unrest so often surges like the waves of the sea.

Prayer: Dear God, thank you for the gift of Your Son Jesus. I invite you Jesus into my heart to fix my brokenness.

Be Lord of my life and live in me for your glory. Amen.

# The Double Rainbow

**M**any years ago, while I was doing a bit of fencing around the sheep fank on the farm where I was born and brought up, a very heavy rain shower poured down upon me. With my waterproof gear on I turned my back to the wind and stood for a few minutes to let it pass. It was torrential for a wee while, and I enjoyed a measure of excitement as the rain pounded on my waterproofs.

The shower began to pass overhead, and the sun gradually came out again at my back.

Against the background of the very black cloud from which the rain had come a very beautiful rainbow began to appear.

My thoughts went to the story of Noah, where God said He would put the rainbow in the sky as a sign of His promise that He would never again destroy all flesh with a flood (Gen. 9: 8–17).

The judgement was passed and would not be repeated.

This led me to think of the judgement of God for our sin that fell on Jesus, "who His own self bore our sins in his own body on the tree" (1Peter 2:24) and blotted out the record of our sins, nailing it to the cross (Col. 2:14), so that there is no judgement for those who believe the gospel (John 5:24).

Jesus Himself, speaking from the cross, said, 'It is finished', and he bowed his head, and gave up his spirit. (John 19:30)

God judged the earth with a flood in Noah`s day and promised never to do it again on the same scale.

God judged Jesus on the cross for our sins. This act will never be repeated.

While continuing my meditation as I gazed with wonder at the rainbow my thoughts went to Revelation 4 where John was in the spirit and found himself in the presence of God who sat on a rainbow-circled throne (v3).

When we see a rainbow whilst standing on the ground, we only see a half-rainbow, but from God's viewpoint the rainbow circles His throne so that there is nowhere He can turn without seeing it.

Because the rainbow is a sign of His covenant, we are assured that God will always remember that the judgement has been executed once for all, both on the earth in Noah`s day and on Jesus on the cross.

Those who have received Jesus as Saviour (Jn 1:12). have no fear of being judged for their sin because God will be forever reminded by the rainbow around His throne that the judgement for sin has once and for all been dealt with by His Son on the cross.

He can never break a promise.

As I continued to meditate the rainbow began to develop into a double rainbow.

I wondered what the significance of this would be, and Job 33:14 came to mind: "God speaks once, yes, twice, yet man regards it not."

God said "Samuel, Samuel" (1 Samuel 3:10).

Jesus said, "Verily, verily" or "Truly, truly I say unto you" (John 5:24).

I believe God is trying to get our attention so we can hear what He has to say.

I said, "Lord, if as in Job 33:14 man regards you not, I am on full alert and thank You for such a wonderful revelation."

Jesus said, "He that has ears to hear let him hear."

# The Haven Goat

The boys called him Sam. He was a likeable fellow. He seemed to be very innocent as he roamed free around the Haven grounds.

No need to keep him tied or penned up in a shed. That would be a shame … so it seemed.

Then we noticed a few problems letting him roam free.

Some of the flowers began to lose their heads in a mysterious way. The lower branches of trees began to be stripped of leaves. Footprints appeared on the new lawn where grass seed had just been sown. It was noticed that Sam licked up some of the seed that wasn`t covered completely. Goat droppings began to appear on the new paving around the new building. The lovely white chips, which decorate the area beyond the paving, started to take on a new look which was not on the original plan. Wee black spots changed what was a beautiful area into a terrible mess.

I very quickly changed the goat`s name from Sam to Sin. I saw the terrible devastation that the goat was causing and likened it to what sin does in a person's life, if it is left unchecked.

Sin makes us enemies of God. It causes us to do things which God hates.

God is the Gardener of our hearts. He wants our lives to be like a well-watered garden (Isaiah 58:11).

Just as I, the gardener for The Haven, was greatly disturbed by the mess the goat was causing, likewise God, the gardener of our hearts, is more than disturbed, He is heart-broken, by what He sees when he looks into our heart which is full of the sins of rebellion, anger, resentment, lies and deceit, to name a few. We all have sin in us. "All have sinned and fall short of the glory of God" (Romans 3:23).

In order to solve the problem of the mess at The Haven a simple solution was implemented.

The goat was removed from the premises and given a new home.

In order for our Heavenly Gardener to solve the mess sin has caused worldwide, because that's how big the problem has become, He had to deal with it Himself.

John the Baptist called Jesus the Lamb of God, who takes away the sin of the world (John 1 v 29).

Unlike the goat at The Haven that made a mess, Jesus came like a lamb to clean up our mess.

He did this when he hung on the cross. God took our sin and laid it on Jesus, and He took it to the grave when He died for us. Because He had no sin of his own, death could not hold Him: so, He rose triumphant and offers us a clean heart, like a clean and tidy garden.

The choice is yours: to continue to live in sin and its mess or invite Jesus into your heart and receive His forgiveness for your sin, and enjoy a clean life, as Jesus keeps you clean day by day.

# Young Calves

**M**any years ago, when I worked on a dairy farm, calves were taken away from their mothers at birth. The reason for this was so that the milk produced by the cows could be sold. The calves would be fed from a bucket with a small amount of their mother's milk for a few days then introduced to powdered milk.

The first milk from a cow after giving birth is called colostrum. It is a very valuable source of food for the new-born calf. It is rich in protein and antibodies which gives the calf good protection against disease etc. The sooner it gets a good feed of this colostrum the better chance of survival it will have. Within two hours if possible but definitely before six or eight because the calf's ability to absorb the nutrients from the colostrum diminishes as time goes on.

The calf is kept, in a small area called a pen. It`s big enough for it to turn around in and jump about a bit but not excessively. It is quite restricted and lies on a bed of straw.

After about five weeks of being housed in this area it is time to move the calf on into a larger pen with much more space and in with other calves of similar size.

When the gate is opened for the calf to come out you would think it would literally jump at the chance to get out of this small space. But no! It has got so used to its surroundings that it is afraid to venture out. A helping hand is needed.

Getting in behind it and sometimes with a lot of pushing the calf is finally out of its pen. The resistance it puts up can be so great that it will stumble and fall in a heap on the floor.

It's been so used to a bed of straw to stand on that it finds it so difficult to stand on a hard surface. Some calves need to be pushed the whole way to get them to the new area.

Once in this new area with all the extra space and a lovely bed of straw, all the trauma of the flitting is forgotten as the calf goes for a race around the pen. Kicking its heels in the air, and sometimes diving into the straw, is a sight worth seeing.

There are a number of points of similarity when helping people.

Some people have been in the same restricted area for so long that the thought of a move to a better place cannot be imagined.

The young calf in its first pen has no knowledge of a better place. It can`t conjure up in its mind anything other than where it is.

Likewise, a person who has become trapped in

a restricted lifestyle may not be able to imagine anything different.

A push or a shove might be needed. Sometimes a calf is carried the whole way to its new area.

Teen Challenge bus work is a good example of helping people out of one lifestyle into a much better one.

Push, shove or carried, whatever it takes, when a person reaches the new environment of rehab, where new clean bedding, good food and new friends are experienced, the joy can exceed that of the calf in its new pen.

Jesus said, Come unto Me and I will give you rest. (Matthew 11:28)

# The Life-Giving Stream

While I was taking a walk in the park, I noticed a pair of swans in the sea just over the fence.

They were drinking water from a stream which flowed down from the hills above the town.

The water was fresh and clean.

The swans had been swimming around in the sea which is salt water and contaminated with all sorts of rubbish and plastic containers.

The swans had the sense to leave the filth of the sea and get close to the fresh water where they could get a good supply of fresh water to drink.

I began to think of the sea, with all its rubbish and pollution, and likened it to the world of sin in which we live.

It`s so easy to become contaminated with the filth of sin in our world. We are surrounded by it. The Internet, TV, magazines –all have the potential to contaminate us. If we are not careful.

We don`t need to get contaminated as the swans prove to us because they are in the contaminated sea and yet stay pure white.

The secret lies in the words of a hymn that came to mind as I thought about this message.

*I thirsted in the barren land of sin and shame,*

*And nothing satisfying there I found;*

*But to the blessed cross of Christ one day I came,*

*Where springs of living water did abound.*

*Chorus*

*Drinking at the streams of living water,*

*Happy now am I, my soul they satisfy;*

*Drinking at the streams of living water,*

*O wonderful and bountiful supply.*

Having, therefore, these promises, dearly beloved, let us cleanse ourselves from all filthiness of the flesh and spirit, perfecting holiness in the fear of God. (2Corinthians 7:1)

The message I was getting, as I watched the swans reach further and further up the stream where there was no mix of fresh and salty contaminated water at the place where they were drinking, was that as Christians we should not live our lives too near the sinful practices of the world.

We should get as close to the source of the living stream which is Christ.

Drink from Him, the fountain which is pure and clean.

We can have all our sins washed away in the stream

and also drink from it.

> Oh Christ, He is the fountain,
> The deep sweet well of love!
> The streams on earth I`ve tasted,
> More deep I'll drink above.
> There to an ocean fullness
> His mercy doth expand,
> And glory, glory dwelleth
> In Immanuel`s land!

# The Meeting Place

**M**arks and Spencer's was the arranged meeting place for a husband and wife doing a bit of shopping in Braehead Centre.

A problem began to emerge as the husband entered the M&S store. It was huge. Where might his wife be? There were at least two floor levels.

The husband began to realise that a more specific meeting place should have been arranged. Too late now to do anything about it.

A quick search all around the first floor and then down the escalator to the bottom floor. No sign of her. Back onto the moving stairs, glancing frantically for just a glimpse of her that would put an end to the fear of never seeing her again.

Then, from the middle of the stairs, as vision of the bottom floor was about to disappear, a sighting was made.

Frantic not to lose her, he felt it take forever for the escalator to reach the top so that a quick descent could be made down the other side.

By the time the husband started his descent the wife

had vanished among the clothing. At least she was there somewhere. Just a quick dart in the direction of the last sighting should be enough.

Yes, there she was, totally unperturbed and unaware of OR uninterested in the trauma the husband had gone through.

She had said she would be in M&S and that was it.

Certainly, a more specific meeting point would be a good idea for a future expedition.

Did you know that our loving creator God, whose name is Love, has arranged to meet you? He has left very clear instructions in the Bible:

"Here I am! I stand at the door and knock. If anyone hears my voice and opens the door, I will come in and eat with him, and he with me" (Revelation 3:20).

It's Jesus who is speaking ... "I stand at the door and knock."

And the door is your heart. That is the specific meeting place. Not a vague rendezvous out there somewhere.

It`s right where you are at this present moment.

Maybe you have never heard His voice before.

It`s a silent voice in the words in the verse from Revelation 3 quoted above.

He wants to come into your heart to bless you with His forgiveness of sins, to give you peace in this troubled world and a hope for the future.

Can you think of a good reason not to ask Him in?

You can stop searching now. You know where He is.

Prayer: Lord open our eyes to see you. Amen.

# The Rescued Crow

T hings at the zoo were going on as normal.

The big grizzly bear was happily munching carrots which were scattered around on the ground in his living space.

His eating was halted when he heard a loud squawking sound which seemed to be coming from the pond next to where he was eating.

He slowly moved over to the edge of the pond where he could see down into it and there, he saw a crow. It was in the water behind a big stone. He reached down and scooped it out from its trapped position with his big paw which was almost as big as the crow.

This enabled it to flutter across to another corner of the pond. It was a very moving scene to watch as crows are not really made for swimming.

The bear strolled along the side of the pond and positioned himself directly above the crow. He then bent down and reached, once again, right into the water with his big paw, and trapped the crow against the side of the pond wall.

Now he was able to reach down and gently catch the

wing of the crow in his mouth and lift it out from the water.

Just as the rescue was about to be completed, the crow in its frightened state, pecked the bear on its nose causing it to let go of the crow. Luckily it was above the floor of the enclosure and not above the water or it would have been back to square one.

The bear strolled back to the carrots as if nothing had happened, and continued where he had left off, eating more carrots.

The crow had landed on its back when the bear had dropped it. It lay there for a good few minutes before struggling over onto its feet.

It stood there staring at the huge Bear. I wonder what it was thinking.

Perhaps it thought it was a dream. That bear could have killed me. Did that bear just rescue me? He has just saved me from drowning. How could I thank him?

We don`t know all that was going on between the bear and the crow, but it is obvious that a great act of kindness was performed on behalf of the crow.

The story is a parable, an earthly story with a heavenly meaning.

The zoo represents the world, where the crow, which represents humanity, falls into the pond, which represents sin.

The crow is destined to die if help is not offered.

The bear, which represents God, is on hand to respond to the cry for help. He has the ability to save.

Whosoever shall call upon the name of the Lord shall be saved. Rom.10:13.

# The Seatbelt

A few years ago, before my wife retired from nursing, she was getting ready to leave the parking lot after her day's work. She noticed an older gentleman driving out before her onto the main road. He had only gone a very short distance when he stopped and put on his seatbelt. He then drove off some distance up the road, followed by a police car. He was pulled over and stopped and accused of driving without a seatbelt. The gentleman said that owing to the stiffness of his joints he found it easier to manoeuvre about in the car park without the belt on, and then put on his belt when he got into a proper position on the road, ready to move off.

No mercy or grace was shown. The Law would not bend. The gentleman was fined. He had broken the law and had to pay and suffer the consequences even for the smallest fault.

I was so thankful for the verse in Romans 6:14b. 'You are not under law but under grace.'

I was reminded too that we have all broken God`s laws, but He has met our need and paid our debt in full Hallelujah. "He cancelled the written code, with its regulations, that was against us and that stood opposed to us; He took it away, nailing it to the cross." (Colossians 2:13–14).

Because God is so gracious and has paid our debt in full, the apostle Paul warns us not to be too casual about it. He says, 'Shall we continue in sin that grace may abound? God forbid.' (Rom 6:1b–2)

I have thought about being very diligent about making sure my seat belt is on every time I venture out onto the road. The Law is watching.

So also to be able to obey God`s laws for our safety on the journey of life we need to put on Christ (Rom 13–14). We need to keep Him on every moment we are awake.

Finally, something else to think about. If we keep Christ on by faith, we will produce fruit for God. The fruit of the Spirit is love, joy, peace, long-suffering, gentleness, goodness, faithfulness, meekness, and self-control; against such there is no law. What freedom – no Law!

# The Sly Old Fox (Part 1)

It was very dark.

Monday evening, fourth of January 2016.

The ducks had been safely tucked up in their shed for the night.

Activities at the Haven were under way, and the evening was going according to plan.

All good things must come to an end so in due course it was time to retire and get off to bed.

Stillness descended over the Centre as everyone drifted off to sleep.

Morning light began to herald in a new day. It was time to let the animals, hens and ducks out of their sleeping quarters and into the freedom of their play area.

It was then discovered that everyone had not drifted off to sleep.

The sly old fox had been out during the night. Perhaps he hadn`t had his Christmas dinner and went on the prowl to see what he could find.

Fortunately, all the ducks and hens at the Haven had been all locked away safely for the night.

Not safely enough, because there were no ducks to be found when the door was opened to let them out.

The sly old fox had dug a tunnel underneath the fence at the back of the duck house.

It emerged nicely into the surprised faces of the ducks.

We can only imagine the terror that came over these birds as the fox attacked and dragged them out and away from their home.

This incident has a serious message for us in our day-to-day living.

The Bible warns us to be self-controlled and alert. Your enemy the devil prowls around like a roaring lion looking for someone to devour. (1 Peter 5:8)

Already he has been very successful in his attacks on staff and residents connected with the Haven.

The devil has lots of tricks up his sleeve (Drugs and alcohol to name a few) to bring us under his power, and some people have lost their lives by falling for them.

The duck house had a fault as was revealed by the fact that the Fox still got in even with the door shut.

However, we have a place of safety, which the words of this lovey hymn reveals:

> *Safe in the arms of Jesus,*
> *Safe on His gentle breast,*
> *There, by His love o`ershaded,*

*Sweetly my soul shall rest.*

Jesus said, "I give my sheep eternal life and they shall never perish; no one can snatch them out of my hand." (John 10:28)

Ephesians 6:10-18 gives good advice to put on the whole armour of God so that you will be able to stand against the devil's schemes.

Be alert. Even at this moment the devil is on the prowl looking for a way to get at you.

Jesus said, "Watch and pray so that you will not fall into temptation. Matthew 26:41

# The Sly Old Fox (Part 2)

One can only imagine the fear and terror that would enter the ducks when they saw the head of the fox appearing up through the ground in the duck house.

Perhaps they would have been unaware of the danger while the fox was digging underneath the fence and then on into the house itself.

Eventually the battle was on. The helpless ducks were attacked and slaughtered. No mercy was shown. They were all dragged out of the duck house and away to their deaths.

We might wonder why God allowed such a thing to happen.

Surely, he could have intervened and saved the ducks.

Let us focus our thoughts on a far more traumatic scene.

King Herod was on the prowl searching for baby Jesus to kill him. (Matthew 2:13)

Mary and Joseph were alerted and escaped to Egypt for safety.

Herod was furious when he discovered that he had been outwitted and commanded that all the boys two years old and under should be killed.

This slaughter was far worse than the fox with a few ducks.

Matthew 2:18 gives some indication of the terror and trauma experienced at the time.

> *"A voice is heard in Ramah,*
>
> *Weeping and great mourning,*
>
> *Rachel weeping for her children*
>
> *And refusing to be comforted,*
>
> *Because they are no more."*

Like a roaring lion or a charging bear, is a wicked man ruling over a helpless people. (Proverbs 28:15)

Be self-controlled and alert. Your enemy the devil prowls around like a roaring lion looking for someone to devour. (1Peter 5:8.)

He tried again to devour Jesus in the wilderness by pressuring Him with lots of temptations, but Jesus put him to flight. (Matthew 4: 1-11)

One day Jesus said, referring to the devil, "The prince of this world comes but he has nothing in me." (John 14:30)

Jesus was a perfect man. He had no sins of his own. The devil had no hold on Him as he has on us. We are like sitting ducks for the devil just like the ducks were for the fox in our story. Helpless to defend ourselves.

Jesus was on a mission. He was on His way to Jerusalem knowing that He was going to suffer and be killed and be raised again the third day.

Peter tried to hinder Him, but Jesus could see that the devil was at work again. (Matthew16: 21-23)

The devil, still prowling around seeking the downfall of Jesus, entered into Judas.

Judas betrayed Jesus and led the band of soldiers to him. Jesus willingly yielded to the enemy because He was on a mission to die for our sins. He could have called for more than twelve legions of angels (72,000) to rescue Him.

There was more horror and terror as Pilate took Jesus and scourged Him. The soldiers made a crown of thorns and put it on His head. They mocked Him and struck Him with their hands. They led Him out to be crucified. (John19:1-18)

Among the crowd that gathered around the cross was Jesus' mother. (John19:25)

As we think of the fox, tearing apart the ducks in the duck house, think of the feelings of Mary as she watched her son being so brutally treated by men stirred up by the devil.

But He was wounded for our transgressions, He was bruised for our iniquities; (wickedness), the punishment for our peace was upon Him, and with

His stripes we are healed. (Isaiah 56:5)

We asked at the beginning of our story why God didn`t stop the fox from killing the ducks. No answer was suggested.

Why didn`t God step in and save His Son from death on the cross?

We have the answer.

God was right there in the middle of it all.

God was in Christ so that He could take the punishment for our sins. (2 Corinthians 5:19)

After Jesus rose again from the dead, He had a talk with his disciples.

He reminded them that his mission on earth was complete. He then gave them instructions. (Luke 24:44-48)

It was a great victory over the devil and not a defeat as might have been thought at first.

Let us take time to think about the horror and trauma of the ducks but let the incident point to the far more meaningful and planned sacrifice of Jesus who gave His life into the hands of the devouring lion, for our salvation. He can rescue us from the power of Satan, the devil, if we ask Him to come into our heart. He is waiting. He is calling.

Hallelujah, what a Saviour.

# The Trees

From inside of the house, I could hear the sound of the wind.

I opened the back door to have a look outside. The wind was very strong, and I could hear it whistling through the trees at the bottom of the garden. They were about twenty feet tall and created a very effective protection against the storm. I had planted them about twenty years ago.

I didn`t realise then how important they were going to be to-day, but I could see now, the great advantage of this wind break.

I was standing in a very calm atmosphere at the back door appreciating the work the trees were doing of stopping the effect of the wind

As I thought about this it made me consider again a tree planted not twenty years ago but over two thousand years ago.

It was the tree made into a cross on which Jesus died. He took our place, the guilty place and died for us.

Not the tree, but Jesus on the tree, shelters us from the storm of the judgement of God for our sins, when we put our faith in Him as our Saviour.

We can then live in the calm of God`s love, mercy, grace and forgiveness.

The verse of a hymn sums it up nicely.

*There rose a keen relentless storm,*

*It burst on Christ alone;*

*It marred His visage and His form,*

*But thus He saved His own.*

*He bore the grief for our relief*

*Unaided and alone.*

"Come to Me," Jesus said. (Matthew 11:28)

Yes, come in out of the storm.

# The Turning of the Tide

While staying on the island of Mull for a few days, one afternoon, I sat by the waters` edge on the South shore of Ben More.

I was feeling a bit depressed and disappointed at my attitude as a Christian.

It was the summer holidays, and our Sunday school was on holiday for a number of weeks but was due start again soon.

I really was not looking forward to getting back into harness again and felt guilty about this, knowing how much Jesus had done for me.

It was while I was weighed down and feeling like this that I sat on a stone right by the water's edge.

I was reading a little booklet called "The Heart at Rest" by Saint Augustine.

The title of the article I was reading was, "Freely, Freely you have received."

It read like this: "Are only those who have not sinned blessed? No, those are blessed whose sins have been forgiven. That grace is given to us freely: we have no good works to show yet He forgives us our sins." (Ephesians.2:8-9, Titus.3:4-5)

I looked away from my book to meditate on those words and discovered the tide was at this very moment beginning to turn. It was starting to retreat.

So, it is in a person's life when the tide of sin begins to overflow the soul, faith in the free gift of salvation, without works, turns the tide. A great release from drowning in sin is experienced.

When the enemy comes in like a flood the Spirit of the Lord will raise up a standard against him. (Isaiah 59:19)

# The White Stone

T he weather was good. I was at Bible camp with around 30 helpers and 30 young people.

The plan was to have a day trip to Millport and cycle round the Island, roughly 10 miles.

A few of the younger members were not confident about riding a bike so I offered to look after one young lad who is connected to the Church I go to.

We set off in the Minibus to Largs (where the ferry takes you over to Millport.)

I kept a close watch on my lad, John (not his real name) to make sure he was safe at all times.

I didn`t want him to come to any harm such as falling overboard from the ferry.

A short bus trip from the ferry brought us into Millport where we hired the bikes.

A suitable one was chosen for us. A bike with a small one attached for John to sit on so that he would rely on me for the lead and support. He had pedals to help with the hard work but I think he preferred to be dragged along and just held on tight.

I began to get to know John as I hadn`t known him before.

I sensed his fear as we started off along the road. He began to call out from behind, "Donnie, slow down, you're going too fast! Keep out a bit, you're to near the edge of the road! It`s too bumpy! Can you not take another road?"

Philippians 4:6-7 says:

Do not be anxious about anything, but in everything, by prayer and petition, with thanksgiving, present your requests to God. And the peace of God, which transcends all understanding, will guard your hearts and your minds in Christ Jesus.

Also Proverbs 3:5-6 says,

Trust in the Lord with all your heart and lean not on your own understanding; in all your ways acknowledge Him and He will direct your paths.

John just had to hang on and trust me to get him safely to our destination, which we did in due course.

Sometimes we might be wondering about the journey we are on.

Too fast. Too near the edge. Too bumpy. Would like a smoother ride.

Perhaps we should just take the Lord at His word and trust Him.

John and I arrived safely at the café on the other side of the island.

There we enjoyed drinks and ice-cream.

Across the road from the café, at the roadside, John found a large white stone. He called it a pearl stone. It was about the size of a small football. He said he would like to take it back home.

I said that I would put it in my rucksack with all our other stuff. I carried everything to let him be free.

That's what Jesus did for us.

Isaiah 53:4-6 says. "Surely He took up our infirmities and carried our sorrows."

When we got back home, I shared with the people in the church my experience with John.

I shared that our time together had brought us much closer together.

I was with him all the way.

Our journey was unique to us.

So, it is on our journey with Jesus. We share all of life`s moments with Him. He is with us all the way.

He said he will never leave us or forsake us. (Hebrews 13:5)

Our journey with Jesus is unique to us.

I showed the people in the Church the big rucksack I carried and reminded them of the burden Jesus carried when He went to the cross and carried all our sins and took the punishment due to us so we could go free. I showed them the white stone which John found. I read Revelation 2:17b.

To him who overcomes I will give him a white stone with a new name written on it, known only to him who receives it.

I suggested to John a name I could imagine on his stone could be LOVE.

When our journey on earth with Jesus is over and we meet Him face to face in Heaven,

The white stone to those who receive it will have a name known only to them.

Rejoice in the Lord always.

# Trees and shrubs

T rees and shrubs were getting too big at the roadside. Vision was getting very limited coming out from the farm onto the main road. Drastic measures were needed to remedy the problem. Every obstacle had to be removed before an accident would happen. So, with hand saw and garden loppers I set about the offending items.

Blood, sweat and tears are some things one might suffer under certain circumstances and although I didn`t experience all three physically they were all there waiting to erupt into full experience.

It was a hot day, and I certainly lost a lot of sweat. Nettles were very much in the way and stings even through my trousers were numerous. It was exhausting work. Sometimes down on hands and knees to crawl under branches to get to the trunk of a tree so that it could be removed from the base so that it would not grow back again.

Eventually the job was done. What a pleasure it was to stand at the exit from the farm road and have clear vision for a great distance, both to left and right directions, making for a safe approach on to the main road where the traffic can be very fast moving.

Many thoughts came to my mind as I meditated on the whole procedure.

Trees and shrubs were getting too big and blocking vision.

Sin is the main problem for us, blocking our vision of God. (Isaiah 59:2)

Drastic measures were needed to remove all the trees etc.

For Jesus to remove the sin barrier between us and God, it cost Him literally blood, sweat and tears.

# The Lamb

Whenever a ewe has a lamb and it dies, the skin can be taken from the dead lamb and placed over an orphan lamb which can then be introduced to the mother whose lamb died. She will smell the scent of her own lamb and will accept it as her own. Usually after a day or so the skin can be removed as a permanent bond will have been established between the mother and the lamb.

Remember God killed animals to make coats of skins for Adam and Eve. (Gen. 3:21)

When Jesus died on the cross His blood was shed for us. He did this for us to deal with the problem of our sins which are a barrier between us and God. (Jn.14:6.) He provided a coat or a cover for us that we put on by faith (Jn.1:12) and God accepts us (Eph.1:6) because He smells the sweet fragrance of Jesus.

When you see the wee adopted lamb skipping and jumping in the field you must remember a lamb died to give it a new life.

Likewise, when we see a sinner, saved by grace adopted into God's family, (Eph.ch.1v5-6) and enjoying a close relationship with Him, we must remember a lamb died to make this possible. The Lamb of God. (Jn.1:29, 1Pet.1:18-19). But remember Jesus rose again from the dead because he had no sins of his own. Hallelujah!

The adopted lamb sometimes finds it strange to be with a different mother than its own, but it soon settles down if it is well fed.

Likewise, God's children who have been rescued from the devil can take a wee while to get adjusted to a relationship with God. But because God is a good and loving God His adopted child can soon settle down as he finds his needs being met. Sometimes it can take longer for this relationship to develop to a total peace on our side but with God it is immediate.

*He has made a full atonement,*

*Now His saving work is done;*

*He has satisfied the Father,*

*Who accepts us in His Son.*

# A Blessing in Disguise

It was a very windy day, and I had a lot of small branches and twigs in piles in different parts of the garden.

I had pruned lots of bushes and it was time to gather up all the cuttings.

I decided to use my barrow to transport those branches to a corner of the garden.

The problem was the wind.

When I piled up a few branches on the barrow, the wind was blowing them off again because it was so strong.

It was then that I had an idea which seemed a bit silly at first but had method in the madness.

I loaded a large heavy stone onto the top of the pile of small branches and twigs to keep them from being blown off the barrow.

I was then able to transport the load safely to the corner of the garden and tip them there.

Although the barrow load was a lot heavier than it would have been without the big stone, it was worth the extra work of pushing the extra weight.

It was a blessing in disguise.

I thought of how we might get a blessing in disguise brought about by circumstances outside our control.

Many years ago, my daughter, while driving my Volvo estate car, veered of the road, rolled down a small embankment and ended up in a ditch, upside down. She was unhurt and managed to get a window open and crawl out onto the grass beside the ditch. The water was flowing freely through the upturned car. She could have drowned if she had not been able to get out.

Help arrived as passing motorists came on the scene and someone brought her home.

When I went to the scene of the accident and saw the car in the ditch, upside down, my first reaction was shock. It looked so humiliating for the lovely estate car to be on its roof with wheels up in the air.

Then as I got closer and looked in through the open window where my daughter had escaped from the car, and saw the water running through where she had been and could have died, but didn`t. A silent voice spoke to me.

I knew it was God because I had entered a relationship with Him before I was 10 years old, by accepting Jesus as my Saviour, and knew His voice. It was a silent communication to me. He said, "I am taking your car, but I am sparing your daughter, but never forget, I didn`t spare My Son, when he went and died on the cross for your sins."

At that point in my mind's eye, I saw Jesus with the crown of thorns on his head. Blood trickling down his face mingled with the spittle of those who spat on Him. He was in a mess. (John 19:1-3)

My daughter only had a wee cut on her finger and a bit of mud on her as she crawled out of the car. God had spared her life.

I said, thank you God for sparing My Daughter and thank you God for not sparing your Son so that we could be saved.

The blessing in disguise for me is that in losing the Volvo, I gained an encounter with the God of Heaven and earth which outlasts any vehicle which will ultimately perish with age.

Can you think of a time when you had a blessing in disguise?

# *A Sad Story*

**K**ara was all set for the big win of £10,000.

She had reached the final in a game "Tipping point"

The game consists of dropping metal discs called counters, about the size of a 50 pence piece, into a machine. The shelf, on which the counters settle, moves back and forward. As each counter settles, the shelf gets overcrowded, and the movement causes one or more to tip over the edge onto a catchment area. Each counter over the edge gets £50 added to the contestant's bank.

Kara, one of four contestants had accumulated £3,000 putting her in the lead.

This gave her the chance to win the Jackpot: £10,000.

To play for this she put a special counter into the machine.

It was a wee bit bigger than the others and had a star on it. If this one could be pushed over the edge £10,000 would be hers.

Counters had to be earned. Questions on various subjects had to be answered correctly to receive one, two or three counters.

Kara had attempted to answer questions from all five categories and had succeeded to get the star counter to the very edge of the shelf. One more counter would be enough to push it over the edge, but she was out of counters.

It was so very frustrating.

So close.

There was one more chance though; Kara could trade her £3,000 which was hers to keep, to purchase another three counters.

Would it be worth the risk? She took the risk. She had seen others do it on previous occasions. Some had won. Some had lost.

Counters drop into the machine in a very random way. They can very often miss the target so that the star counter remains where it is.

Kara traded her £3,000 and purchased another three counters.

The first one into the machine pushed passed the star with no movement.

The second one did the same. Tension had mounted to fever height.

Only one counter needed to push that star over the edge and £10,000 would be hers.

She now had that counter in her hand. It would get her the £10,000 or nothing.

Into the machine it went. It slipped passed the star with no movement.

A great sense of loss entered the room.

What might have been had been lost.

Kara went home with nothing. She could have gone home with £3,000 but the chance of £10,000 was a chance she was willing to take and so lost everything.

Jim Elliot, an evangelical Christian said, "He is no fool who gives what he cannot keep to gain that which he cannot lose.

John Ch. 3:16 Says, "For God so loved the world that He gave His one and only Son, that whosoever (that means you) believes in Him should not perish but have eternal life."

To believe, or not to believe. What's at stake? It's eternal life or eternal death.

Kara had a dilemma. Trade, or not to trade. She traded and lost. It was only money.

Jesus asked, "What shall a man give in exchange for his soul? (Matthew ch.16:28.)

Judas sold Jesus for thirty pieces of silver. (Matthew 26:4-16)

Eternal life, or eternal death?

Jesus guarantees eternal life to all who come to Him and accept Him into their hearts.

You can't lose. There is no risk.

Your eternal destiny is at "Tipping Point "on the balance.

Will you accept, or Reject Jesus?

# Porridge

I lit the gas and slid the big porridge pot over the flame.

Water and a little salt had been added to the oats some time earlier.

Five minutes passed and it looked as if nothing was happening in the pot.

A little stirring of the contents of the pot and a bit more patience while the gas continued its work of bringing the pot to the boil. Eventually there was evidence of something happening.

There were bubbles popping up here and there in the pot showing that it was beginning to boil.

A certain length of time was needed to allow the raw oats to cook and become soft and ready to serve for eating.

The whole procedure led me to think of a person who has been introduced to the gospel message.

At first there might not be any evidence of anything happening but as the Holy Spirit begins to work in the heart, and conviction of sin troubles the person, changes begin to appear.

Questions are asked about how to get right with God and instructions as how to accept Jesus as Saviour and forgiveness of sin is in the mix.

The process can take some time but, like the porridge, a gradual change takes place which the Bible calls the 'new birth' which happens when Jesus is accepted into the heart by faith.

The person has become ready, not to be served like the porridge, but to serve his Lord and master Jesus.

Ready to introduce others to the saving power of the Gospel.

The gospel in a nutshell is,

'For God so loved the world, that He gave His only begotten Son, that whosoever believeth in Him should not perish, but have everlasting life.' (John 3:16)

Printed in Great Britain
by Amazon

84920278R00047